Mexican Independence Day and Cinco de Mayo

Dianne M. MacMillan

Reading Consultant:

Michael P. French, Ph.D.
Bowling Green State University

—Best Holiday Books—

Enslow Publishers, Inc.

44 Fadem Road	PO Box 38
Box 699	Aldershot
Springfield, NJ 07081	Hants GU12 6BP
USA	UK

Acknowledgments

The author would like to thank Mark Wasserman, professor of Latin American history at Rutgers University, for his careful review of the manuscript. Thanks also to Araceli Tinajero, Spanish linguist at Rutgers University, for providing the Spanish pronunciations in this book.

Copyright © 1997 by Enslow Publishers, Inc.

Library of Congress Cataloging-in-Publication Data

MacMillan, Dianne.
    Mexican Independence Day and Cinco de Mayo/Dianne M. MacMillan; reading consultant, Michael P. French.
       p. cm. — (Best holiday books)
    Includes index.
    Summary: Provides background on the people and events that are commemorated on two important Mexican holidays, Independence Day and Cinco de Mayo, and describes how these holidays are celebrated.
    ISBN 0-89490-816-2
    1. Mexico—Social life and customs—Juvenile literature. 2. Independence Day (Mexico)—History—Juvenile literature. 3. Cinco de Mayo (Mexican holiday)—History—Juvenile literature. 4. Cinco de Mayo, Battle of, 1862—Juvenile literature. 5. Juárez, Benito, 1806-1872—Juvenile literature. [1. Independence Day (Mexico) 2. Cinco de Mayo (Mexican holiday) 3. Holidays—Mexico. 4. Mexican Americans—Social life and customs.] I. Title. II. Series.
F1210.M23 1997
394.26972—dc21

                                   96-47244
                                       CIP
                                       AC

Printed in the United States of America

10 9 8 7 6 5 4 3 2 1

Illustration Credits: D.J. Lambrecht, p. 15, 21; Frank L. Lambrecht, pp. 16, 36, 37; Diane C. Lyell, pp. 8, 13, 18, 19, 20, 24, 44; Dianne M. MacMillan, pp. 6, 7, 17, 22, 32, 35, 38, 40, 41, 42, 43; James R. MacMillan, pp. 4, 31, 34; Steve Strickland, p. 30.

Cover Illustration: Diane C. Lyell

Contents

Boys and girls scream with delight as they enjoy the many rides on Mexican Independence Day.

Celebrate!

Boys and girls scream with delight as they zoom down the high hill of a roller coaster. Ferris wheels turn round and round. On a stage, a group of children are dancing. The girls wear red and green full skirts. The boys have on white cotton pants and large white shirts. Red sashes are tied around their waists. On their heads are wide-brimmed hats called sombreros (som-BRAY-ros). The children twirl and stomp their feet.

Thousands of people have come together. There is music, talking, and laughter. Teenagers walk by, eating long, sugar-coated churros (CHOOR-ros).

People sell serapes and purses at a sidewalk stand.

A band is playing and singing. Many people sing along. The sidewalk is lined with decorated booths. People sell hats, a kind of shawl called serapes (sa-RAH-pays), and baskets. There are also food booths. Delicious smells of tacos (TAH-cos), burritos (boor-REE-tos), and enchiladas (en-che-LAH-dahs) fill the air. They

People sell serapes and purses at a sidewalk stand.

A band is playing and singing. Many people sing along. The sidewalk is lined with decorated booths. People sell hats, a kind of shawl called serapes (sa-RAH-pays), and baskets. There are also food booths. Delicious smells of tacos (TAH-cos), burritos (boor-REE-tos), and enchiladas (en-che-LAH-dahs) fill the air. They

Celebrate!

Boys and girls scream with delight as they zoom down the high hill of a roller coaster. Ferris wheels turn round and round. On a stage, a group of children are dancing. The girls wear red and green full skirts. The boys have on white cotton pants and large white shirts. Red sashes are tied around their waists. On their heads are wide-brimmed hats called sombreros (som-BRAY-ros). The children twirl and stomp their feet.

Thousands of people have come together. There is music, talking, and laughter. Teenagers walk by, eating long, sugar-coated churros (CHOOR-ros).

are made from thin, pancakelike pieces of bread folded around beans, meat, and cheese. Children line up to buy Mexican pastries and cookies. These people are celebrating an important Mexican holiday.

Families have come together to celebrate. All of this excitement is part of Mexican Independence Day. In many ways, it is similar to the Fourth of July in the United States.

Mexican Independence Day is celebrated on September 16. The date in Spanish is diez y seis de septiembre (de-es ee SAY-ees day sep-ti-EM-bray).

It is hard to decide which Mexican cookie to buy.

It is an important day for Mexican Americans. In the spring on the fifth of May, cinco de mayo (SEEN-co day MAH-yo), another celebration takes place. Cinco de Mayo remembers a special day in Mexican history.

These two days bring Mexican-American families together. Everyone is proud of their history. Let's find out more about these holidays.

The red, green and white colors in the costume worn by this girl are the colors of Mexico.

Mexico

Many Mexican Americans were born in Mexico. The country of Mexico is south of the United States. At one time, much of the land in the southwestern part of the United States belonged to Mexico.

Thousands of years ago, many cultural groups of native peoples lived in Mexico. Some of the largest groups were the Mayas (MAH-yahs), Toltecas (tol-TAY-cahs), Zapotecas (zah-po-TAY-cahs), and Aztecs (az-teks). They lived in large cities. The cities had beautiful artwork and buildings. The Mayas and Aztecs built pyramids using stones.

In 1521, soldiers from Spain came to the New World. They conquered the people of Mexico. All of the land became a Spanish colony. The Spanish called the colony "New Spain."

The Spaniards made the Native Mexicans learn to speak Spanish. Spanish priests taught the native people Christian beliefs. A priest is a leader in the Catholic church. For three hundred years, the country was under Spanish rule. Everything made or produced went to the Spanish king. Native Mexicans were not allowed to govern themselves except on a local level. Many could not carry guns or ride horses. Everyone had to pay heavy taxes.

The people were very unhappy. They wanted to make changes. No one knew how to begin. They needed a leader to take charge and rally the people. Father Miguel Hidalgo became that person.

Mexican Independence

Father Miguel Hidalgo (me-gal e-DAHL-go) was a Catholic priest. He was well liked and a good speaker. Father Hidalgo was born in a small town one hundred miles north of Mexico City in 1753. Mexico City was the capital of New Spain.

Miguel's parents were Spanish. His father was in charge of a large estate or hacienda (ah-see-EN-dah). Miguel was the youngest of four boys. He was a very good student and studied hard.

After graduating with honors, he became a priest. For many years, he taught at a college. Father Hidalgo read many kinds of books. He read about freedom and democracy. He believed that all of the people of Mexico should be free to govern themselves. He thought the Spanish rulers were wrong to treat the Native Mexicans so badly. His ideas got him into trouble. He was removed from his teaching job.

In 1803 Hidalgo was sent to the small town of Dolores. There he served as a parish priest. The Native Mexicans of Dolores were very poor. They were forced to work long hours in the silver mines. The work was dangerous. Many times the walls of the mines caved in, and Native Mexicans were killed.

Others worked in workshops or in the fields of the large haciendas. They had little food to eat. Their homes were small and crowded. What little money they earned went to the landowners to pay rent.

Father Hidalgo wanted to make life better for the Mexican people. He tried to help them set up small businesses. Some wove cloth. Others made wine or raised honey. The Spanish rulers closed the businesses down.

Father Hildago used his home as a

schoolroom. He taught many Native Mexicans to read and write. He tried to get employers to treat the Native Mexicans better. However, Father Hidalgo could not change the attitude of the Spanish rulers.

The only way there could be changes was to overthrow the Spanish government in Mexico. On September 16, 1810, Father Hidalgo began ringing the church bells. The people heard the

Father Hildalgo wanted to make life better for the poor Native Mexicans.

bells. They left the mines and fields and came to the church.

Father Hidalgo shouted to the people to rise up against the Spanish rulers.

No one wrote down Father Hidalgo's exact words. People remember some of the things he said. "Long live our Lady of Guadalupe! Down with bad government! Death to all Spaniards!" The Lady of Guadalupe was another name for the Virgin Mary, the mother of Jesus. Native Mexicans loved the Virgin Mary. They believed she appeared to a Native Mexican many years ago in the 1500s.

Father Hidalgo's cries for freedom were called the Grito de Dolores (GREE-to day do-lor-ays) or the Cry of Dolores. Native Mexicans were moved by Father Hidalgo's words. They grabbed picks, shovels, pitchforks, and other tools to use as weapons. They made banners with pictures of the Virgin Mary on them. Carrying the banners, they began to march through the streets of Dolores. They were ready to fight for their freedom.

Traditional Mexican music helps people remember the struggle for independence.

Parades are a part of Mexican Independence Day celebrations.

First they attacked the silver mine. Then they charged a stone fortress. When the fortress was destroyed, the people began to attack the haciendas. The Spanish soldiers were outnumbered by the huge crowd of Native Mexicans.

As the people marched, more and more Native Mexicans joined the fight. In a few weeks, more than eighty thousand people had joined with Father Hidalgo. The Native Mexicans no longer feared the Spanish.

However, the Spanish troops were very strong. After a few small victories, Father Hidalgo's followers were defeated. A year later in 1811, Father Hidalgo was captured and put to death. Still, the Native Mexican people would not give up. Father Hidalgo had given them hope. They continued to fight for their freedom. It took eleven more years. Finally in 1821, Mexico won its independence from Spain.

The Mexican flag has three stripes: green, white, and red. Each color stands for a different idea. Green stands for independence. White stands for religious freedom. Red stands for unity.

Each year on September 16, Mexican people everywhere remember Father Hidalgo. He is called the Father of Mexican Independence. Church bells ring in honor of this man. People repeat his famous speech, the Grito de Dolores.

Cities with large numbers of Mexican Americans have many activities to celebrate Mexican Independence Day. Parades are popular in California, Arizona, and Texas. Thousands of

Important members of the Mexican-American community ride in cars in the Mexican Independence Day parade.

These girls celebrate in traditional Mexican costume.

people line the streets to watch. Mexican-American community groups march down the street. There are marching bands. Famous Mexican Americans from sports, entertainment, and politics ride in cars and wave to the crowds.

Some people carry the Mexican flag. The flag has three large stripes: green, white, and red.

Everyone likes to watch Mexican folk dances.

Each color stands for a different idea. Green stands for independence. White stands for religious freedom. Red stands for unity. In the center of the flag is an eagle. The bird stands on a prickly pear cactus plant. In its mouth is a snake. According to a legend, the Aztecs saw an eagle eating a snake. They built their capital on

While trumpeters play, a dancer dressed in an Aztec costume waits to perform.

Traditional food like tacos, and burritos are part of Mexican Independence Day, and every other day as well.

that spot. Mexico City was built in the same place as the Aztec capital.

On Mexican Independence Day, people like to watch folk dances. Dance is an important part of Mexican culture. Culture is the way people dress, what they eat, the music they play, their beliefs, and their customs.

The dancers wear colorful costumes. The women wear brightly colored long, full skirts with ruffles. The skirts swish and swirl as the women dance. Male dancers wear a rodeo-rider costume called a charro (CHAR-ro). Some men wear sombreros. Dancers twirl and stamp their feet to the beat of the music. Some of the dances are very old. Many of them are based on ancient Native Mexican stories.

Some dancers dress in Aztec costumes with lots of feathers. The dances tell about gods and emperors. Dances help Mexican Americans remember their Native Mexican heritage.

The Mexican hat dance, called jarabe tapatio (hah-rah-bay tah-pah-TEE-o), is the national dance of Mexico. The dancers take quick hopping steps around a sombrero that is placed on the floor.

Carnivals, street fairs, and celebrations held in parks are other ways Mexican Americans celebrate Independence Day. Green, white, and red balloons decorate booths. Paper flowers made from tissue paper are tied to fences and poles. Everywhere there are the smells of delicious Mexican food. Some people sell tacos, burritos, enchiladas, rice, beans, and menudo (may-NOO-do). Menudo is a soup or stew. Many families bring their own food and have a picnic. In the evening, fireworks often burst across the sky. Everyone remembers the brave men and women who struggled for Mexican freedom.

Tacos are everyone's favorite meal.

Benito Juárez

After Mexico gained independence in 1821, the country needed new laws. A new government had to be formed. This was not easy to do. The Mexican people had very little experience. Spain had controlled everything.

Native Mexican soldiers, who had fought against the Spanish, were the first ones to control the government. Then other groups tried to take control. For forty years, control of the government shifted back and forth between different groups. Civil wars broke out between the two main groups. The government was weak. During this time of weakness, United States and

Mexican troops clashed in a border dispute. On May 12, 1846, the United States declared war on Mexico. Two years later the war ended with Mexico's surrender. As a result, Mexico lost its territories in the United States. This land became the states of California, Nevada, Utah, Arizona, and New Mexico.

Benito Juárez (bay-NEE-to hoo-AR-ays) was a Zapoteca Indian. He was born in 1806. His parents were poor peasants. Both of them died when Benito was three years old. He was raised by grandparents and later an uncle. At age thirteen, he moved to the city of Oaxaca (wa-HAH-ca). He worked for a man who was a bookbinder. Benito could not read or write. His employer liked Benito and adopted him. He helped the boy learn to read and write. Benito studied very hard.

When he grew up, Juárez became a lawyer. He was very smart and honest. The government tried to take away land that belonged to Native Mexicans. Juárez helped the people protect their land. He defended poor people in court.

In 1841, Juárez became a judge. Six years later he was elected governor of the state of Oaxaca. While governor, he built roads and schools. Everyone knew about his honesty.

Meanwhile, civil wars between government groups were still going on. People were tired of the fighting and killing. Many people thought that Juárez might be able to make the country stronger. They hoped he could bring about peace and unity. In 1860, the people elected Juárez president of Mexico.

Battle of Puebla

President Juárez had a big problem. The Mexican government owed a lot of money to other countries. One of the countries was France. If Juárez paid the money, there would be nothing left in the treasury to help Mexicans. He chose to use the money to help his people.

This angered Napoleon III (Louis Napoleon), the ruler of France. Napoleon III decided to invade Mexico and make the country a French colony. Napoleon III's army was the strongest and best trained in Europe. In December of 1861, the French army attacked Veracruz (VAY-rah-croos),

Mexico's largest port city. The people in Veracruz surrendered to the French.

Then the French began the four-hundred-mile march to Mexico City. They planned to capture the capital and take control of the government. On May 4, the French army camped near a small town called Puebla (poo-AY-blah). The town was halfway between Veracruz and Mexico City.

The Mexican general, Ignacio Zaragoza (ig-NAH-see-o sah-rah-go-sah), tried to stop the French forces. Outside the city of Puebla were two hills. Zaragoza placed most of his soldiers on the hills. General Zaragoza did not expect to win. Many of his men had been soldiers for less than three months. Others knew nothing about fighting against well-trained soldiers. The Mexicans had crude weapons. Zaragoza only hoped to slow the French invasion. He wanted to give President Juárez more time to fortify the capital.

The French attacked on the morning of May 5, 1862. They stormed up the hills. Brave Mexicans fired muskets (old-fashioned, long-barreled guns) and cannons. Many of the French soldiers were driven back down the hills. Then it began to rain. The slopes of the hills turned into mud. It became difficult for the French to advance. After four hours, the French gave up the battle. They withdrew back to Veracruz. The small ragged group of Mexican soldiers had defeated the powerful French army.

A year later, the French tried again. This time they succeeded. The French army captured Mexico City. Napoleon III made an Austrian

Many enjoy celebrating the Mexican victory at Puebla.

Every May 5, thousands of people come together to celebrate the Mexican victory over the French at the Battle of Puebla.

archduke, Maximilian, the emperor of Mexico. For the next five years, the Mexican people fought the French. Benito Juárez led the fight. The victory at Puebla gave them courage and spurred them on. If they could defeat the French once, they could beat them again. In 1867, the Mexican people succeeded. They overthrew Maximilian. Napoleon III removed all his troops from Mexico.

Once again Juárez became the leader of the country. He brought about reform and many changes. He is remembered as one of Mexico's greatest presidents.

This great president made Cinco de Mayo, which is Spanish for May 5th, a national holiday. He did not want people to forget the brave men who fought against the French. Every May 5, Mexican people remember the victory over the French at the Battle of Puebla.

Celebrating Cinco de Mayo.

Getting Ready to Celebrate

Mexican Americans love parties and celebrations. They call them fiestas (fe-es-tahs). Fiesta also means "feast day." A feast day to Mexican Americans means music, dancing, colorful clothes, and good food.

Some women make their own tortillas (tor-teel-lyahs) which are flat, pancakelike bread made from corn or wheat. But most buy their tortillas at the store. Tortillas are eaten every day and fixed in many ways. They can be wrapped around meat, cheese, beans, and rice. Frying or baking tortillas in different ways will make tacos, enchiladas, or burritos. Cheese and sauce

Fiesta means "feast day" and celebration.

are put on top of many Mexican dishes. Every fiesta means eating delicious traditional food.

Often mariachi bands play at fiestas. The bands are a symbol of Mexico. The band groups generally have six to eight members. There are usually two men that play the violin. The others play trumpet, guitar, and bass. They sing and play favorite folk songs and popular music.

Some folk songs like "La Cucaracha" (lah coo-ca-RAH-chah), which means "the cockroach" in Spanish, have been sung for hundreds of years.

Mariachis dress in colorful costumes trimmed with silver buttons that flash in the sun. They often wear hats called sombreros. Some people believe mariachis date back to the time when the

These women are frying tortillas.

Mariachi musicians are part of Mexican celebrations.

French army occupied Mexico. Many French soldiers married Mexican women. They hired small bands to play at their weddings. The bands were later called mariachi because the French word for wedding is "mariage."

Whether this is true or not, everyone loves listening to the mariachis play. They are an important part of every celebration.

Many schools have special Cinco de Mayo celebrations. At a school in Orange, California,

Everyone loves listening to the mariachis play.

Boys and girls decorate school fences with paper flowers for Cinco de Mayo.

boys and girls put on a special Cinco de Mayo school fair. For weeks they plan for the big day. Some of the children learn Mexican songs and dances. Everyone helps make decorations for the school playground. Parents cook Mexican food. The excitement builds until the fiesta of Cinco de Mayo begins.

Cinco de Mayo

On Cinco de Mayo, the playground is crowded with children and their families. Many boys and girls walk in a big circle while music plays. On the ground numbers are placed around the circle. Mexican music blares from the loudspeakers. Who will stop on the lucky number? The music stops. The walkers stop and look down at the numbers. Laughter and shouting greet the child who is standing on the winning number. The child wins a cake.

Over to the side, there are games like "Lasso the Bull." Each player has wooden rings. The rings are tossed at the horns of a paper bull. To win a prize, a ring must hang on the horn. Nearby are food booths. Children and their parents line up to buy tacos.

Tree trunks and school fences are gaily decorated with tissue paper flowers made by the boys and girls. Mexican-American children share their culture with one another. They enjoy telling other boys and girls about the Battle of Puebla.

Other Cinco de Mayo celebrations take place

One lucky child will win a cake.

These children are playing "Lasso the Bull."

at parks and churches. There are many events: picnics with piñatas (pen-YAH-tahs) for the children, puppet shows, baseball and soccer games, and carnivals. Museums have art shows. They display paintings and artwork created by Mexican Americans. Everywhere there are mariachis and folk dancers.

Many Mexican Americans look forward to celebrating Cinco de Mayo with their friends and

Children decorate tree trunks with paper flowers to celebrate Cinco de Mayo.

neighbors. They enjoy eating Mexican food and going to fiestas. Cinco de Mayo has been celebrated in the United States for over one hundred years. Mexican Americans enjoy Cinco de Mayo. However, they consider Independence Day as the most important Mexican patriotic holiday.

Mexican Americans are proud of their history. Mexican Independence Day and Cinco de Mayo are important days to remember. Both holidays celebrate the courage of the Mexican people.

People enjoy eating Mexican food and going to fiestas.

They remind everyone that no matter how great the struggle, it is important to keep trying. Mexican Americans look forward to next year's Mexican Independence Day and Cinco de Mayo. Olé (O-lay)!

These dancers perform a traditional folk dance.

Glossary

bass—A large violinlike instrument that plays low notes.

charro—A rodeo-rider costume worn by male dancers.

colony—A territory that is far away from the country that rules it.

culture—The arts, beliefs, and customs that make up a way of life for a group of people.

custom—A tradition practiced by many generations of people.

fiesta—A Mexican celebration.

hacienda—Country estate owned by a rich Spanish landowner.

heritage—Traditions and beliefs passed down from earlier generations.

mariachi—A band of six to eight members that plays Mexican folk songs and popular music.

menudo—A type of soup or stew.

piñata—A hollow, treat-filled papier-mâché figure broken during Mexican celebrations.

pyramid—A huge stone structure that is square on the bottom and has four sides shaped like triangles.

sombrero—A wide-brimmed Mexican hat.

tortilla—A flat, pancakelike bread made from corn or wheat.

Index

M

Maya, 9
Maximilian, 31, 32
Mexican Flag, 17, 19-21
Mexican Independence Day, 8, 17, 18, 23, 29, 43, 44
Mexico, 9, 10, 21-22
Mexico City, 11

N

Napoleon III, 28, 31

O

Oaxaca, 26

P

Puebla, Battle of, 29-30, 31, 40
Puebla, Mexico, 29, 31, 32

S

sombreros, 5, 23, 35
Spain, 10

T

Toltecas, 9

U

United States, 25, 26

V

Veracruz, Mexico, 28-29, 30
Virgin Mary, 14

Z

Zapotecas, 9
Zaragoza, Ignacio, 29